DOWNLAND

DOWN

A farm and a village

Roger Coleman

LAND

Introduction by Robert Rodale

Edited and designed by David Larkin

A Studio Book   The Viking Press   New York

First published in 1981 by the Viking Press (A Studio Book)
625 Madison Avenue, New York, N.Y. 10022

Published simultaneously in Canada by
Penguin Books Canada Limited

Library of Congress Cataloging in Publication Data
Coleman, Roger, 1930–
    Downland: a farm and a village.

    (A Studio book)
    1. Burpham (Sussex)—Social life and customs.
    2. Farm life—England—Burpham (Sussex)   3. Coleman,
Roger, 1930–   I. Larkin, David.   II. Title.
DA690.B955C64   942.2′67   81-50433
ISBN 0-670-28116-6   AACR2

Printed in the United States of America

THIS BOOK IS TYPESET IN *Bodoni Book*
AN EARLY TWENTIETH-CENTURY
ADAPTATION OF GIAMBATTISTA BODONI'S
1771 DESIGN. IT WAS ONE OF THE
FIRST 'MODERN' TYPEFACES HAVING A
MORE ACCENTUATED STRESS AND
RELATED CLOSELY TO THE COPPERPLATE
STYLE POPULAR IN THE EIGHTEENTH
CENTURY.

Contents

Introduction 6

Preface 8

Map 13

Splash Farm 14

Winter 17

Spring 45

Summer 79

Autumn 113

Little Down 136

Introduction

In *Downland*, Roger Coleman has written and painted a personal reaction to what is, basically, a personal situation—a small farm and the village connected to it. He has given us a vivid image in three dimensions. First, because he is primarily an artist and sees with a special eye, he uses the dimension of sight. By exercising his remarkable visual sense and artistic talent he gives us a pure, uncluttered view of a particular farm. Every aspect of Splash Farm jumps to the eye, in broad strokes, and in rich detail. Because it is a small farm, the picture is intimate. There is nothing impersonal about it. We are brought into direct contact with the land, with the plants, the animals, the machines, and the people.

To the purely visual interpretation, Coleman adds the human dimension, and in a very powerful way. We get to know the farmer, George Field, and his family, as real people, not as stereotyped images. Farmers, perhaps more than any group, have been classified as being all of a type—laconic hayseeds, one and all. Actually, they and the members of their families are as individualistic as other people. The sensitive and affectionate writing about George Field and his wife Libby, no less than their extraordinary, strong portraits, allow us to know them as friends, better than if their personalities were expressed in one medium alone.

All these features combine to form a view that will be surprisingly new to many people—Americans have a stereotype about farms too, a hazy mental image composed of maple syrup and green hills (set somewhere in New England) or a picture of endless, unbroken square miles of waving wheat (mid-West). We may also remember smudge pots and vast orange groves.

But Roger Coleman's vision of the farm landscape in the South Downs is hardly stereotypical. There are no traditional pastoral scenes here but a series of dramatically realistic views of the landscape at work. He does not avoid the sight of the tractor, the shed, the fence; indeed he celebrates their relationship to the earth, their integral role in farming life.

It is important that we know the real people, in their real setting, because farm people, as varied and as fascinating as people the world over, can be understood clearly only in an ecological as well as a personal sense. They are part of the web of life of their farms, and we need to sense the outline of the web to get a feel for who the people really are.

So we come to the third dimension of this beautiful book: the Village of Burpham, a village that has grown up amidst the small farms that surround it.

6

The village is important, its people diverse, the pattern and the rhythm of its life the product of the work the people do day-after-day: there are an enormous number of skills represented in any group of people who run small farms—animal husbandry, knowledge of the land and growing things, conservation, sanitation, fencing, drainage, building, and not by any means the least, a great skill with machines. All these are visible in this book, and beyond that there is an awareness of how these varied people fit into their personal landscape, the bringing of schoolchildren to the dairy farm to see how cows work, the patient participation in village celebrations, all making up a community of spirit that binds a diverse group of people together. The village community exists because small farms exist. As individual farming re-establishes itself on the landscape so will villages.

Finally, and cleaving to the quality which makes Coleman an artist, he moves us through the seasons of a farm and a village. And this is extremely important. The ninety-seven per cent of us who no longer are farmers need to know that winter does more to a farm than kill annual plants and cover the land in snow. We should understand how the lives of farm people are changed by the seasons far more than are the activity patterns of city folk. Looking ahead to try to sense the outlines of our own future, I see tremendous value in having a real sense of what small farm and village life is like. The years ahead are going to limit our physical world. Many thousands of new people enter our world each day, yet the amount of land for farming remains static, and the number of farm people continues to decrease. Perhaps a time will come when the real value of the land will be forced upon us, when the deeper values of a lifestyle we seem to have turned away from will become vital to survival itself. Farms will become more important in that time, their ability to thrive and produce inevitably an issue for public debate and policy action.

The land and our dependence upon it are the same the world over. The beauty that the book *Downland* provides is self-evident; the closeness to the farm and the village that *Downland* provides is likely to be of profound usefulness.

Robert Rodale

Preface

Nearly eight years ago, my wife Louise and I moved to Burpham from the centre of London—just a few yards from Oxford Street—with rather unfocused expectations and for a combination of reasons, none of them particularly urgent. The idea of escaping the city to paint untainted nature was certainly not among them although I did not rule out the notion that painting the landscape might be agreeable. We both enjoyed the country, Louise as a one-time resident and user (she owns two horses) and I as a tourist, dating from the time when, as a boy during the war, family holidays were spent in the West Riding of Yorkshire, Derbyshire and Wales, among other places. My attitude then to the country could be expressed happily by the epigraph to the first movement of Beethoven's Sixth Symphony, "Awakening of pleasant feelings upon arriving in the country."

We decided finally on Burpham after considering various places, the farthest away being Brecon in South Wales. I say "decided" but that implies a rational process; as with many things in life, there was a strong element of fortuity in it. A family friend of Louise's was married to one of the farmers in Burpham and through them we were first acquainted with the place and also notified when the house we now live in came on to the market.

As I said, my expectations were vague. Whatever notions of country life I had—apart from the impressions gained from holidays and stays with friends—were limited to those I had garnered from such diverse sources as *Cider with Rosie*, *Cold Comfort Farm*, the novels and poems of Thomas Hardy, Gilbert White, and others both widely divergent and diffuse. I suppose I expected life to be friendlier in some way than in the city, less hectic obviously, less anxious—in fact all the commonplace impressions. As do many Englishmen, I felt, for no reason, that I was at heart a countryman, not from experience but as a sort of birthright through some specifically bucolic gene we all possess, providing us with the capacity to adapt to rural life without learning. (Actually I was not born or brought up in a town, nor in a suburb, but in an industrial village in the Midlands with easy access to slightly soiled fields, spinneys and miles of muddy canals.)

While my ideas of the country were ill-defined, if kindly disposed, I don't think they were superstitious or sentimental as are those of some towndwellers. Often the urban attitude to the country is one of almost automatic unthinking superiority—a superiority nevertheless tinged with fear. Townsmen have always sallied into the countryside with silly ideas of its inhabitants and their ways which evidence to the contrary does little to modify. Such ideas revolve around the belief that the countryside is Eden or some version of paradise. Admittedly, compared with some city centres today, a great deal might seem like paradise, but that is no excuse to misconceive the characters and attitudes of the people who work on the land. For example, in the eighteenth century, the poet James Thomson exulted

The house
at Splash Farm

in the notion that farming was "happy labour, love and social glee," the sentimentality of which, though in less rapturous tones, persists today. Something of this is found in the view of the country as basically a refuge. It is indeed a refuge. But it is other things as well and it is not a museum.

The most earnest invasions of the countryside in recent years have followed very positive renunciations of town, career and social life for a life of self-sufficiency and simplicity. Many people do want to escape from what they see as the increasingly less agreeable aspects of urban life—the growing complexity, declining services, dirty streets, plastic food, "blessings" of planners and games of architects, the noise, smell, the general rat-race and so on. While I felt increasingly less sanguine about living in London, for us there was no hint of hysteria and no vocation to live the "natural" life as it were. Being an artist, I could, all things being equal—which of course they were not—work as well in one place as another. I did not see myself at all on a par with, say, the advertising executive who gives up, if not fame, then probably fortune, to cultivate green peppers and keep goats. My intention was uniquely to move from one place to another and to carry on working as I had in London, albeit in vastly pleasanter surroundings.

Quite what kind of social structure I expected to find I cannot remember, if indeed I expected anything at all other than the vague fiction that almost every citydweller can draw upon from one source or another.

In fact I found in this small community of some 250 people living either in Burpham or its neighbor Wrepham, a wider variety than might be imagined. Not in any significant order, but just as they occur to me, the community is made up as follows: farmworkers and their families and the people who also work for the Norfolk estate but not on the land, those who work in London during the week and come down to the village at weekends and for holidays, one or two others who have businesses or who are employed in the neighborhood (Arundel, Littlehampton and Worth); and quite a large number of retired business or professional people most of whom come from London. Hence there is considerable diversity both in occupational background and in age levels.

I heard a man on the radio the other day talking about the influx of middle-class people from town to village, particularly in the South of England. His point was that this influx was undermining the very life these people were coming to the village to find. Quite what it is they are undermining I am not sure, but surely the point is that the "traditional" village life all we urban expatriates dream about has been changing because of the developments in farming, which presumably started with the concentration of energy on this sector during the Second World War. These changes are far too many and detailed to go into here but generally they can be summed up in the statement that fewer and fewer men with more sophisticated machinery cultivate larger and larger acreages. Not only does a relatively small number of men actually work on the farms—over the centuries the very essence of village existence—but also the crafts which supported pre-mechanized farming have disappeared. Burpham is unusual in having a village blacksmith but he is in reality a part of the leisure industry and not of agriculture.

In addition to the list mentioned, there is a small selection of self-employed entrepreneurs including an antique furniture restorer, the local shop, the George & Dragon, the blacksmith, the vicar—who shares the village with an appointment at Lambeth Palace—and myself.

During an initial period of six months which, because of the silence, the darkness, the inexplicable noises and lots more, was pure novelty and consequently absorbing, I found it very difficult to adjust. This was mainly, I think, because the society I frequented in London was (and I didn't realize quite how much until I left it) largely professional. Most of the people I knew well were, if not artists in the technical sense, involved in what are called creative occupations—television, journalism, architecture and so on—and I missed the sense of community based on shared assumptions of, say, the value of the work we did. The other aspect of life in London of which I was not really aware until I moved away from it was that you seldom knew your neighbors. You saw them at the gate, or passed them on the stairs, acknowledging one another with a nod and a word. While your neighbors were near strangers, your friends lived miles away in Highgate or Knightsbridge or Barnes or Islington. But gradually, and through the discovery of the landscape and the difficulty of trying to paint it, the transition from town to country occurred almost without my realizing it.

Our family holidays, particularly those spent in the West Riding of Yorkshire when I was a boy, represent the awakening of my interest in landscape—nothing to do with art, all I drew then were Spitfires and Lysanders I remember. Over the years those fells and dales of Yorkshire have taken on an idyllic character and I still carry around their idealized image in my head. Against this I seem unconsciously to assess the quality of other landscapes. What I rejoiced in, and still do, was the long, even contour of fells against the sky and the open continuous nature of the terrain, hillside overlapping hillside. I can only suppose that it was the contrast the dales provided with the landscape of small, neat, tightly enclosed—and, I thought, rather boring—fields around my home that was the initial source of their interest to me.

The first time I saw the South Downs was later, in the 1950's—not the Downs around here but at Ditchling near Brighton. The impact they made was immediate. My experience of the dales had been in a similar way almost proprietorial.

Between these two events the aesthetic element had been added to my awareness of landscape. Among the painters whose work excited me when I was an art student was Paul Nash and it was through his paintings that I became aware of the so-called chalk uplands of South England and their archeological remains such as Avebury, Maiden Castle and Silbury Hill. My interest was concentrated on the latter, since I did not know the landscape at first hand (a situation remedied by the Army during my National Service). Not only do I love the configuration of chalk hills, but also I am fascinated by the use that man has made of them over the centuries and the two elements are conflated in my mind. Gilbert White, the eighteenth century naturalist, wrote, "I think there is somewhat peculiarly sweet and amusing in the shapely figured aspect of chalk-hills, in preference to those of stone, which are rugged, broken, abrupt and shapeless." He went on to say that he never contemplates the Sussex Downs "without thinking I perceive somewhat analogous to growth in the gentle swellings and smooth fungus-like protuberances, their fluted sides, and regular hollows and slopes, that carry at one the air of vegetative dilation and expansion." I know of no better description of the Downs than this, or certainly none which accords so closely with my own feelings. I cannot imagine a time when they will cease to provide me not only with inspiration, if that is the word, but also with joy and solace.

Around Burpham

The scenes in this book attempt to bring together the outlines of a particular kind of land and the living it produces. The drawings and paintings were done over a period of roughly a calendar year, from January, 1979, to January, 1980, and include the landscape in and around Burpham in West Sussex together with portraits of some of its inhabitants and subjects from the working life of a farm. I have made no effort to be definitive—indeed, that would take many volumes—but to create rather a series of impressions with a linking motif of scenes from Splash Farm and of George and Elizabeth Field, the tenant and his wife: and finally, to unite the whole through the march of the seasons, always of paramount importance to those who live on the land.

Edward Lear, the nineteenth century artist and poet, described the road to Burpham as a "road to nowhere." A rather superior view, perhaps a townsman's, and certainly inaccurate, for "nowhere" suggests the exhilarating remoteness of moorland. Burpham is not remote in that sense, lying just three miles off the main trunk road between Eastbourne and Southampton. The reality is that the road is a cul-de-sac giving access to the villages of Warningcamp and Wrepham, with Burpham at its end.

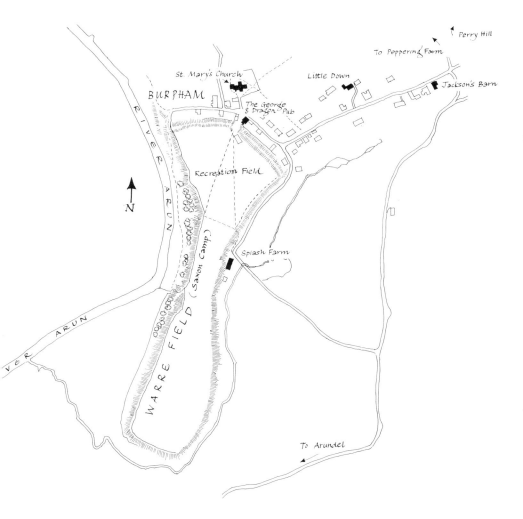

Standing on a chalk scarp above the river Arun, people seeing Burpham for the first time invariably describe it as beautiful, but compared with many Sussex villages the architecture is not outstanding. It has no really distinguished building; the church is functional rather than beautiful—indeed the three lancets in its east end seem to be designed rather to keep out the wind from across the Downs, which it overlooks, than to illuminate the interior—and the houses individually reflect the dictates of economics more than the character and charm of some traditional Sussex country cottages. What makes the place so attractive is its landscape; not simply the Downs, but the closer landscape of the situation of the buildings collectively in their setting. So Burpham emerges as a small village of unselfconscious beauty and astonishing tranquility; one of those rare places where time can appear to pass slowly and without complication.

The stream rising near Jackson's Barn flows, when in spate, under a steep bank crowned with ash and the bleached, barkless remains of once magnificent elms now looking more like stone than wood—plinths for pastoral sculpture—below the main part of the village to Splash Farm and then on its course down the valley. The road beyond Jackson's Barn is straddled by the village—houses, a small hotel, more houses, one village shop and, at its end, Lear's 'nowhere'—a small square accommodating the church and the George & Dragon pub. From the square, past the pub, a path leads to a long plateau

13

of land above the valley floor known as Warre Field. On the Ordnance Survey maps this tongue of land is marked as "fort", recording it as the site of a fortification from which Burpham gets its name. The promontory is said to have been one of Alfred's strongpoints against the incursions of the Danes in the ninth century. Today, any conflict the old battle site witnesses is confined to cricket, for it is village recreation ground and home of the Burpham and Warningcamp Cricket Club. The remainder of the plateau is farmed by George Field. The whole promontory stands, on its west side, about fifty feet above the river to which the drop is almost vertical, a solid chalk bluff overgrown with old-man's-beard, ash, thorn and elder. On the east, George's side, the scarp is lower by twenty feet or so, listing like a ship's deck.

Burpham is, of course, first and foremost a community of people—people of varied occupations, lifestyles and interests, although farming dominates the area. And there are some who have retired from city life to the village, attracted by its tranquility. But for all its variety, Burpham is a unified community with its own calendar of events and social occasions, its own unpredictable dramas and excitements. For all its outward calm and apparent lack of activity, a year there is as full and fulfilling as any I have experienced elsewhere. . . .

Splash Farm

Splash Farm itself is a dairy farm of some 118 acres, the larger part of which lies between the Arundel to Burpham road and the river Arun. Most of the land is flat, crossed by drainage ditches but nevertheless flooding at rainy times. In addition to the main acreage, there are a further eighteen acres up at Warre Field.

The farmhouse and buildings are hard against the bank of this promontory on its eastern side. It is difficult to estimate the age of the house itself, two hundred years perhaps, but changes in brickwork are evidence of constant addition and modification. An earlier building on the site is said to have been a mill and this was allegedly referred to in the Doomsday Book. The site of the buildings is cramped between the bank and the stream which is responsible both for the form of the promontory and the name of the farm. The farmhouse itself is in the traditional downland idiom of flint and brick and red clay tiled roofs.

looking down over the roof of Splash Farm

looking down over the roof of Splash Farm

Winter

Jackson's Barn

A typical representation of Winter, such as you would find on Christmas cards, consists of a photograph of a clump of conifers against an impossibly blue sky with only slightly less blue shadows reaching across a crisp, white tract of virgin snow. An image of this kind is a good example of the tendency we have to sentimentalize nature just as Christmas cards generally sentimentalize Christmas in order to transform the most unacceptable season into something more benign, even friendly. We all know of course that Winter seldom conforms to the above ideal and when it does provide the

18

ingredients the discommodiousness outweighs the charm, except of course for children and those adults who have an easy access to rosy memories.

The real characteristics of Winter in this country are that it is soggy, gloomy and raw—not crisp, bright and cold: it is a period when nature's (and our own) more generous impulses are in abeyance. Consider the life-enhancing qualities of an average day in early February—dark, damp, cold; a day, as it were, that starts late and never recovers; a day that requires the electric light from beginning to end. Is it any wonder that it is the spirit which suffers rather than the fingers? You can, after all, take precautions against the "wrathful, nipping cold." Not long after undergoing such a day as this I came across some lines of verse by W. E. Henley in which he talked of "winter's grey despair" which seems to me to be a pretty good way of putting it. Winter really does seem able to bring us close to a kind of despair on occasions. For me those occasions are brought about not by cold nor storms but by bad light, quite apart from the fact that bad light makes it hard to see when you are painting. Under conditions like these it is not hard to resist the indulgence of reverie. Indeed it seems characteristic of Winter, certainly in northern countries, to induce in people a feeling of suspension to parallel, as it were, the state of suspension that the land itself is undergoing. The body has not much choice but to endure the rigors but the mind can be off on its own, engrossed in (to quote the subtitle of Tchaikovsky's First Symphony) "winter daydreams." Whether or not it was winter when Goethe wrote his poem "Kennst du das Land" I do not know but the yearning it expresses for the land where lemons grow and where the senses and the spirit can thrive suggests that it was.

In spite of this, however, Winter does have many compensations, particularly for artists. Oddly enough, until the impressionists or thereabouts, painters did not bother much with Winter; it was generally the time they spent in the studio, working-up the sketches and drawings made in Spring and Summer into large exhibition pictures. I cannot believe artists such as Constable or Cotman would be blind to the possibilities of say, snow, so the conclusion must be that there would have been no market for such views. Now, of course, snow is the most appealing aspect of Winter for the painter. The first fall of the year is always magical, not simply as a visual experience but also as it rekindles something of the excitement and joy we experienced as children. However much people complain about its inconvenience and its hazards, there is a part of them that is, if only for a few hours, exhilarated by the transformation before them. And a very thorough transformation it is; a reversal, virtually, of the tonal values of the landscape when the earth becomes as light, if not lighter, than the sky and the objects—trees, bushes, fences, become vignetted, isolated from their usual context, framed and separated.

George in the dairy

George Field is a true native of Burpham. He was
born 46 years ago in the same farmhouse where he
now lives with his wife Libby, daughter Sally and
son Nicky. Apart from his National Service with the
Royal Sussex Regiment in Germany, he has spent
all his life in and around the village. His father and
his grandfather (a great man with horses by all
accounts), were tenants of Splash Farm
before him. For most of his adult life George
worked alongside his father, until the latter's
death four years ago.

Libby

George filling hopper
with fertilizer

The first impression I had of George was one of
quiet affability and directness—nobody's fool but a
man prepared to meet the world more than halfway.
Watching him at work around the farm, he appears
to have a sort of unmethodical practicality. His
workshop next to the farmhouse suggests he is not a
tidy man—indeed the atmosphere of Heath Robinson
lingers among the assortment of spare parts, tools,
fishing tackle, bicycles, nuts and bolts, string and
so forth. I remember an occasion when he and
Arthur Binfield (who helps him on a part-time
basis) were repairing the combine which was
discovered to be seriously defective just as it was
about to be put to use. George carried out the repairs
with a mixture of improvisation and common sense,
patience, cups of tea and laughter.

George is a serious and conscientious man,
certainly a serious farmer. But his propensity for
laughter is very evident. Consequently he is one of
the best people I know to whom to tell a funny story.
He is also a tolerant man, and even-tempered. His
wife Libby, a much more volatile person, once
complained that his inability to lose his temper
could drive her crazy. As far as I can tell, he is
unenvious, uncovetous and, in the obviously mildly
pejorative sense, unambitious. But pride he does
have, particularly in his herd of 70 or so cows.
Insomuch as one person can say that another feels
this or that, I would say that George Field was a
happy man.

Feed for cows awaiting milking

George Field shaking out a hay bale in a fodder rack in the yard prior to the afternoon milking—as he does every morning and afternoon whatever the weather.

The needs of animals take no account of seasons or weather. Cows may spend the winter days inside for the most part, but they still have to be fed, and milked twice a day.

The land, on the other hand, lies sleeping under snow, or waterlogged, or frozen hard like the steppes; outdoor life is suspended, the crops planted in the autumn waiting in the cold ground for better times.

Mick Standing

30

But, in most winters, days without snow outnumber those with it; the year dealt with in this book, however, was luckily exempt from that rule. Nonetheless, there are bright days in winter, clear, hard and cold, when the air is thin and the horizon is sharp enough to touch. Such days are as marvelous as snow. The low sun in that clear air produces the long shadows of a dream and reveals the texture and swell of the earth to an archeologist's satisfaction. I know that people feel that green in the landscape is the color of life and growth, but you can, or rather I can, get tired of it. A colleague of mine complained of painting in the Summer—". . . too bloody much green about," he said. These bright days in Winter with their assortment of greys, dark reds, ochre, raw siennas, are a splendid antidote to green. . . . As I look out of my window I can see the near-white of a ploughed field, the rich raw sienna and pinkish ochre of a row of bushes along a field bank and the silver-grey of dead nettles punctuated by the dark greens of ivy, holly and ilex. That is Winter as well as "grey despair."

I said earlier that the winter landscape, on account of its neat bare aspect, can seem an empty and lonely place. On the other hand modern farming methods, which enable fewer and fewer men to work larger and larger areas of land, see to it that the landscape at any time of the year presents a somewhat deserted appearance.

Those of us not directly involved in agriculture tend to think of it in a light more romantic than, for instance, the operation of our own mundane jobs. Farmers, whatever miseries they believe they undergo, do have the aggravation of earning their living from a commodity, i.e., the land, which many thousands of others, often unconnected with rural life, consider in some way to be theirs, something in which, by birthright, they have a share. We who were not brought up in rural surroundings and who have worked for many years in the city, cling to a mish-mash of notions of what the country should look like and of what the bucolic life is essentially constituted; most of these notions are nostalgically inclined and historically inaccurate and garnered from a multiplicity of sources that beggar listing. But in the last analysis for most townsmen who enjoy the countryside, to live and work there represents some version or other of Eden.

My conception, for instance, is that the relationship between man and the landscape on which he works is necessarily an idealized one in which industrious, happy, healthy people go about their elemental tasks with enthusiasm, joy, and when the going gets irksome, if it ever does, endurance.

What is amazing is that in spite of direct evidence to the contrary, these simplistic beliefs continue to feed the senses. For example, I came across an

Edwardian photograph recently representing a harvest scene, in which in a moderately sized field at least twenty-five people of both sexes and all ages were involved along with four horses and carts. My imagination seized on this image of communal effort and filed it in a mental compartment labeled 'rural life'—along with innumerable others from memories of potato picking as a schoolboy during the war to Thomas Hardy, from Harvest Festival hymns to glimpses from the window of a train, and from *The Waltons* to Robert Frost. It hardly needs saying that harvest time today resembles that photograph not at all, but it nonetheless stays in my mind as a kind of paradigm, on a level not greatly affected by common sense, of how things "ought" to be.

So, most landscapes today are depopulated Winter and Summer alike (of course some always have been but the context here is this and similar parts of Southern England). Paradoxically though, in terms of men standing on the land, doing something directly to it, it is Winter activity that approaches the essentials of the harvest photograph rather than that of Summer. Millet's "sower" now rides a tractor and wears earpads, and Stubbs's horses have become as mechanized as a tank squadron. Because nowadays farm work is carried out by machinery the relationship between its operators and the land must be different from and less intimate than that which existed for the unmechanized predecessors. I don't mean to say they know less now or that they are less expert— they know different things and

their expertise is technical—simply that they actually stand on the earth less, move about it on their feet less and the operations they perform on it are indirect and not by hand.

Winter Work

In Winter then, when the chilled ground is indifferent to human ministrations, attention turns to the chores of maintenance—fencing, ditching, hedging, repairing gates and holes in the road, things of that kind; and it is for things of that kind that you have to come down from the tractor cab and get earth on your hands instead of oil.

Richard Snow, manager of the Peppering Farm (with his back toward us) and Mick Standing, one of its tractor drivers, are making a drain to carry away slurry from the stockyard. I have always been interested in the postures of men working and in the effects that work and wear have upon clothes. Both aspects show up well in the cold, clear February air.

All farm machinery is marvelous to draw and
machines in the landscape have been a preoccupation
of mine since my student days. Here the JCB is
ditch digging on Peppering Farm.

One very cold and clear February
morning after the first snow had gone
and before the second arrived, I came
across John Binfield and Ned Johnson
from Peppering Farm rewiring a fence on
the high ground above the valley.
Standing, as they were, against the Downs
on the other side of the river, in bright
morning light, they presented something of that
ageless, demanding and functional relationship of
man and the earth.

The Road to Arundel

It has been said (by Walter Pater constantly) that all art aspires to the condition of music, presumably meaning that it seeks to be abstract and self-contained rather than imitative of the real world, and that the word "constantly" implies that it cannot or should not (Pater was not to know that it did) ever completely succeed. There is, then, a tension between the facts of one's subject, what the eye sees (quite literally, no two individuals ever see anything exactly alike), the paint, the surface, the medium, etc., and what is represented by them. This is a tension of which I am very conscious.

The marks made to test a wash, say, or the residue of wash left on the palette, have a quality that seldom gets into the picture, or if it does, it is by an accident which is subsequently muddied by anxious endeavor. But the abstract element too is very apparent in the downland landscape itself—the large rhomboid shapes of the fields, textured but even, fit together in a marvelously satisfying way. I always start a painting with such a paradigm in my head but then I see, say, tiremarks of a tractor rounding a copse and become involved in both the detail and its significance. This process is illustrated in the picture of the road to Arundel.

The field is a rather sparse crop of winter barley, dun-colored after the snow, although I have emphasized the greenlessness considerably. Over the shoulder of the hill, amongst dark leafless trees, is the hamlet of Wrepham and there are two traces of lingering snow.

The Dryer Lane

At the northeast end of the village, where the road from Arundel turns into the village street, a track, in effect a continuation of the street, leads off into the open downland. This track is variously known as Middle Lane, the Chalk Road, and, to the workers of Peppering Farm, the Dryer Lane, after the grain-drying barn which stands half a mile or so along it.

The first walk we took after we had moved to Burpham was along this track, for the simple reason, I suppose, that it is both accessible and inviting. One is immediately off the tarmac of the street and on to two ribbons of chalk, which in dry, fine weather seem literally to be pure white, separated by a band of green, and which drive straight and flat between a low gappy hedge for a hundred yards or so. Then the ground rises and the hedges thicken up along steep banks on either hand and from the declivity thus created no view of the landscape to the front or to either side is possible. From the lane's entrance the effect of this short rise is to conceal its subsequent direction and character, making the track doubly enticing.

The two views of Dryer Lane are separated by about three months. The snow was the first of the winter and under it the hedges are the dominant feature; now the white road, which, illuminated by a watery late March sun, contrasts sharply with the dark green rows of winter barley.

Perry Hill

"Blunt, bow-headed, whale-backed" is how Kipling described the South Downs, adding in the next stanza of the poem, "Clear of officious fence or hedge half-wild and wholly tame . . ."

Kipling would be surprised and horrified today if he could see just how many fences criss-cross the once open spaces. However, he was probably thinking more of East Sussex where he lived, for woods increase progressively westward. Indeed, Constable, when he painted around Arundel, described the woods as 'the chief glory of the place.' But a great deal of the downland has changed from the open spaces on which flocks of sheep cropped and turned to vast rectangles of barley and wheat. While preferring the former I can accept the latter as part of the many changes of habit and method that life constantly demands. Even so, in spite of the ploughing and the fences, the Downs remain 'wholly tame' and, even more paradoxically, 'half-wild.'

I have drawn and painted Perry Hill more often than any other feature, man-made or natural, in the district. Since I came to Burpham it has been of abiding interest to me not only to look at but to walk upon. While it is the most noticeable piece of the immediate landscape, it can hardly be described as noble or dramatic or awe-inspiring or steeped in the kind of mystery that surrounds ancient places such as Cissbury Ring or Chanctonbury, just a few miles away over the Downs; nor, at under 400 feet, is it high. It does, however, fulfill Kipling's description

and, while that might be reason enough for my obsessive interest, it also holds for me an indefinable quality, a magic, that attracts me to it both as a place to be and as a subject for a painting.

I find flat landscape (apart from marshes and estuaries) generally rather dull, perhaps because there is too much sky, too much bright evanescence and not enough ground except as a receding plane. The value of rising ground is that you are presented with earth as theatre almost, something you look directly at, not over. But such notions are technical. They may help to explain why I like to draw a place but not why I like to be there. My somewhat immoderate love of Perry Hill extends beyond poetic quotations and those qualities that appeal to the subconscious to a more practical interest and one that embraces most of the chalk uplands of southern England.

Chalk, more than any other geological substance, records impressions made by man; not just the intentional ones like the Cerne Abbas giant or Uffington's White Horse, but those marks made unconsciously by feet, ploughs and tractors by way of agriculture, trade or habit. The path up the side of Perry Hill, its wild side, a steep uncultivated scrubby pasture festooned with the tracks of grazing animals, is known locally as the Leper's Path because in the Middle Ages, it is said, lepers used it on their way to receive communion through a tiny window in the chancel of Burpham Church. To me the truth of this is not important, only that it has been in use for

a long time and its white scar seems like an extension of the past into the present. Such marks give scale to a landscape, not just a physical scale but another, historical perhaps, archeological, anthropological maybe, probably a fusion of all three.

Perry Hill has its present day landmarks as well: the mile and a half gallops of the Duke of Norfolk's racing stables and a new plantation of saplings, called the Norfolk Clump, to commemorate the late Duke Bernard.

41

Jackson's Barn

The first building in the village street is a flint barn known as Jackson's Barn (after an earlier occupant of the adjacent house, itself once a farmhouse). Despite its position at the opposite end of the village, the barn belongs to Splash Farm. George Field, the tenant, uses it as a barley store.

I made a drawing of it on New Year's day after the first snow of the winter. It seemed part of the landscape itself, almost as if it had always been there. At the same time its elementary proportions and the simplicity of its construction appeared to be an embodiment of the virtues of a less self-conscious and less anxious age than ours. There is substantially small difference between the barn and the Church.

Winter to Spring

The transition from winter to spring in England is a gradual process. The two views of Jackson's Barn that follow, and the trees and bushes around the Vicarage garden, attempt to illustrate not the transition itself but a before and after; the first is of a January afternoon—bleak, wet and cold. For some reason I cannot name, while doing the drawing, the Henry James story *The Turn of the Screw* kept coming to mind; in contrast, the second study is on a May morning. The view is a little way along Dryer Lane, looking back toward the village. The Arundel road comes in at the extreme left.

Spring

Louise and the children

One afternoon in March, Louise and I and our two daughters, Katie, aged four, and Hannah, eighteen months, went out into the paddock at the back of our house where Louise stables her two ponies. It was, I remember, the first day that did not suggest that winter was a permanent condition and, while not being warm by absolute standards, it seemed so in contrast with the unusually long spell of hard weather we had been suffering. There was even a faint, very pale and watery sunlight, "an earnest of the Spring." These studies of Louise and the following drawings originated that afternoon.

The two children had just recovered from whooping cough and had not been out very much since Christmas. Katie had been far more affected than Hannah. Presumably being older, she was more frightened by the bouts of coughing and her confidence in general suffered. Most children are conservative, I have been led to understand, but Katie I suspect is more so than most. Her nature seems contemplative rather than active (the opposite of her sister). Going for a walk, without some exciting objective such as the village shop, is not really her notion of pleasure—consequently to wander round our paddock seemed like a very poor alternative to the fireside and play school.

While Hannah stomped about, falling over, laughing, examining the ground, grinning at the ponies in their boxes, Katie stood at the gate complaining bitterly, saying she wanted to go home, as though home was miles rather than yards away. After some persuasion from Louise, she joined us with rather bad grace and eventually even managed a pale brave smile.

These two versions of the same picture were the result of an attack of caution and sentimentality. In the first I became increasingly bothered by the redness of Hannah's complexion—nor was it soft enough. So in a second version I postponed the problem and started with Katie. A few days later Hannah came in from a walk, glowing a bright scarlet—looking like the abandoned drawing.

In the middle of March George turned out some
in-calf heifers on the lower end of Warre Field
beyond the fence with the water trough. Every
morning and afternoon they were fed hay. They
could do no damage to the field as it was soon to be
ploughed.

54

Ploughing

Ploughing is one of those jobs, like making bread which is of course related to it, or casting a net upon the waters, that is of the deepest significance to the human race and which is one of the demonstrations of the continuity of history. Almost everybody carries an image in his head of the horse-drawn plough with gulls cascading down to the turned furrow, against a backdrop of bare trees, rooks and pale winter sunshine, as described by Edward Thomas in his poem *The Head Brass Flashed out on the Turn*. This is the very stuff of people's dreams of rural life, the idea of honest toil that goes a long way to be self-rewarding. It is also the image that causes pubs the length of the country to sell bread and cheese under the title of Ploughman's Lunch which, in our local—the George & Dragon—for instance, is just about all right, but it is a bit comical across a bar in the Elephant & Castle, say, or Salford.

Our reverence for ploughing is very deep. Yet I cannot imagine our sentimental expression of that reverence going down very well with Thomas Gray's ploughman—celebrated in the opening lines of the famous *Elegy*—who with two horses could plough an acre a day. Ploughing then was a continual process stretching from harvest through the winter up to the end of Spring. Nowadays, to supply the supermarket shelves among other things, that task can be accomplished with tractors in a few days. But when watching George's brother ploughing the lower end of Warre Field on a bright spring morning, I still get a strong sense of the timelessness of this ancient skill.

George Field's brother, Fred, ploughing on Warre Field. The plough is raised out of the ground as the tractor turns at the end of the furrow. The ash tree is growing from the bottom of the bank and only the middle and top branches festooned with old man's beard are visible.

56

Tractors

Tractors, and the machinery to go with them, are a part of the landscape today, an accomplished fact that has been in existence for many years. I know that recently there have been reports and plenty of talk about a resurgence of horse-drawn ploughs and the like, but until the oil runs out altogether, such ventures will be specialist and consciously conservationist. I regret, or rather the romantic part of me regrets, the passing of horses as a source of power; I like painting them and I wish we could see them in the fields. I can imagine that working with them was a far more enriching experience than working with a machine. But that's easy for me to say since I don't have to walk behind them. A short while ago, I was talking to two retired farmworkers, both of whom worked with horses. They said if they had to sit all day in an air-conditioned cab, they would expire from boredom—give them horses every time! "But what about getting wet?" I asked. "Never noticed it," they said, but I bet they did. On the other hand, their affection was genuine and it didn't rain every day.

Many people, particularly those whose background is urban, tend to see the landscape in 19th century terms, without tractors, without machinery, prior to any kind of modernization, to make of it a rustic scene at some earlier stage of development as, for instance, Andrew Wyeth does in his paintings. If there is any model for English rusticity to follow, it is oddly enough Constable. I say "oddly enough" for if there was any painter who observed the facts of the farming of his day and understood its real nature, it was Constable. What, on the other hand, he would have thought of a tractor is anybody's guess. I suspect, from what he said about other aspects of landscape, that he would have taken it in his stride. For example, "I never saw an ugly thing in my life, for let the form of an object be what it may—light, shade and perspective will always make it beautiful," and, "the sound of water escaping from mill-dams etc., willows, old rotten planks, slimy posts, and brickwork, I love such things. As long as I do paint, I shall never cease to paint such places." It has been said of him that he preferred painting man-made canals to mountain brooks, and dams to waterfalls. Not only did he prefer the cultivated to the wild, he represented the up-to-date farm implements of his time with meticulous care. For me, as I suspect it would have done for Constable as well, light and shade render the tractor if not exactly beautiful, as much a part of the landscape as ever his haywain was.

View from the garden of Splash Farm with Perry
Hill in the background.

60

Warre Field with the gable-end of Splash Farm on
the extreme right. Field banks hold a great attraction
for me, mainly I think because of the associations
with the great earthworks of the past. But it is also
something to do with the contrast between the
cultivated areas above and below with the rough
texture of the bank itself.

Looking northeast across the Arun Valley with the
corner of Warre Field embankment in the foreground.
The course of the Splash stream is in the foreground.

The southern end of Warre Field seen from the
Arundel road. Splash Farm is situated out of sight
below the trees in the centre. Its fortlike character
is evident.

I do not often paint long distances—not that this picture of the Arun Valley takes in all that much, but it's a lot for me. I am not really very interested in that hazy conjunction of land and sky, of earth and heaven. I prefer to be reasonably close to what a painting portrays which is another reason why the Downs suit me so well—the scale is small.

A view of Peppering Farm in the distance,
across the Arun Valley and the loop of the river.

65

The paddock behind
and above our house

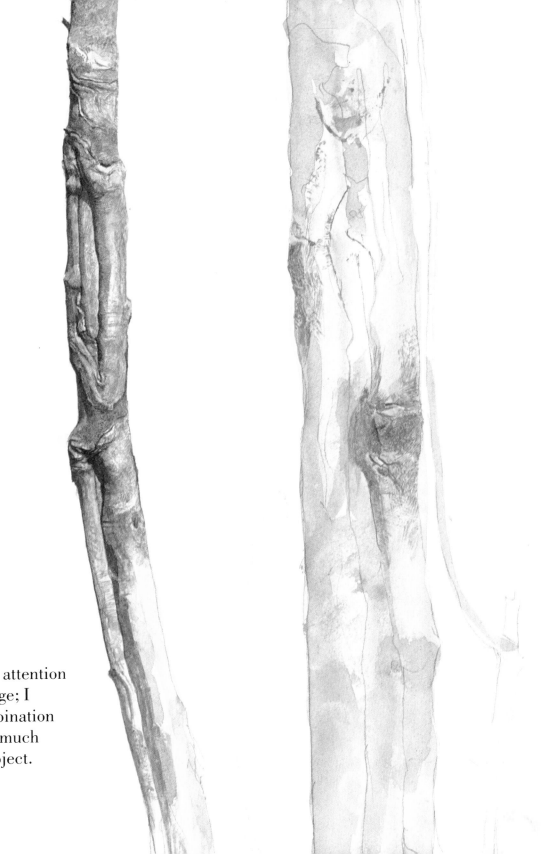

I was in our paddock one morning and my attention was caught by two ash saplings in the hedge; I liked their pale grey/green color and combination of smoothness and contortion. Also, after much landscape, they gave me a "close-up" subject.

Sending a calf off for rearing

The Visit

William Cowper wrote in a poem called *Town & Country* that "God made the country, and man made the town." It is the kind of statement about the relative merits or otherwise of urban and rural life that people have been making for centuries. Cowper's view is very unambiguous—only in the country is one capable of having a decent and pleasant existence whereas the town is synonymous with corruption. We may not be as extreme as he was at the end of the 18th century, or as certain that man's hand was absent from the landscape, but what he says is enshrined in what amounts to folklore—for example, ideas of retirement to a country cottage with roses around the door, or departing the rat-race for rural self-sufficiency. Why I quoted Cowper, however, was not to air the subject generally but because his lines came into my head when I was trying to organize my thoughts about a visit some school children made to Splash Farm. These children brought to my mind some other children who came to our part of the world as evacuees from London forty years ago at the beginning of the Second World War. It was always said that if you asked a Cockney child, presumably also one from Liverpool or Birmingham, or any large town, "Where does milk come from?" the answer would be "Out of a bottle." It was also said that the evacuees had never seen a green field or a cow. So, in Cowper's terms, they had never seen the handiwork of God and only the scruffier end of God's creatures, and he would argue that the deprivation of "natural" sights would lead inevitably to some sort of spiritual undernourishment.

In the 1940's those young evacuees from the streets of big cities represented the biggest gap imaginable between town and country. Yet only the other day there was a farmer on the television saying that, in his opinion, that gap was wider now than it has ever been. Not that the children who visited Splash Farm were from a rundown inter-city area—they were from the largely middle-class seaside settlement of Rustington. Cows they had seen, if only on television, and green grass certainly. None, however, had ever seen animals in a working context. In one of the pictures I have done the teacher is exchanging glances with a cow and it occurs to me that in that look, there is something of the deep suspicion of the countryside that Evelyn Waugh put into Mrs. Salter's mind in his novel *Scoop*.

The children were allowed into the milking parlor four or five at a time while the remainder looked into barns, the insides of tractors and at hens and puppies. Inside the barn, in the warmth, a small group of children watched in silence as udders were washed and milking cups put in place. They seemed awed by the proximity to such large beasts swishing their tails and serenely munching on the hay.

Suddenly, one of the cows emptied its bladder with explosive force. As the steaming urine splashed onto the floor and streamed into the drains, the children shrieked and giggled in forbidden delight.

Milking that afternoon was not George but Alfred Tester who has worked on the farm for fifty years—first for George's father and, since the latter's death, for George. The conjunction of childhood and age, innocence and experience, is eternally interesting. Two of the pictures demonstrate two ways of looking at this subject. The first, a backview of Alfie Tester, was really about the white of his coat and the "white" of the reflections in the wet barn floor. At the same time, however, I was aware of the French critic—the friend of Degas—Edmond Duranty's injunction that "by means of a back we want a temperament, and age, a social condition to be revealed." Whether that ambition has been achieved is not for me to say.

In the second picture, the interest was fairly centered on the story, the contrast between childhood and age—a young hand scratching a supple leg as against an old hand stiffened as it were by use and experience.

Until I came to do this book, the only animal I had
drawn or painted was the horse with its immediate
appeal to the imagination. The cow, on the other
hand, is not an elegant animal and has none of the
association of valor and profit that the horse enjoys
but, when I was forced to consider it, I found to my
surprise that it was a fascinating study and very
exciting to draw with the combination of big smooth
shapes and sharp angular and awkward projections.

Spring to Summer

Our climate, it hardly needs saying, is not a model of predictability. All we can ever be sure of is the general cycle of change—Spring, Summer, Autumn, Winter. At any time we can be assailed by almost any kind of weather so that one year is never exactly like another. Such uncertainty, of course, has its disadvantages, particularly for farmers—or for anyone in fact who works the land for his living. But it has advantages too; it has enriched our language, affected our literature and art and is never boring. Also it provides the principal subject for most casual conversation—very useful between strangers, on trains, in pubs, at parties and so on—non-controversial, of no practical value, but of abiding interest.

For me personally, the odd days are fascinating and welcome; I get a profound enjoyment when some item or other of the weather appears mysteriously inappropriate to the time of year, as, for instance, a high wind on a dull but warm day in high summer which churns the dark, heavy foliage (exploited marvelously, I remember, by Antonioni in his film *Blow-up*). Or a dark, misty, Spring morning—not a mist that will soon clear, but a dense damp one bringing, as it were, January into collision with the bright greens and yellows of April.

It also has to be said that a season often relieves its predecessor so reluctantly that it appears there will be no change at all—just a gradual and not terribly noticeable reduction or increase in inclemency. In a typical year—but I have implied this does not exist so in, let us say, a less eccentric year, the transformation of Spring into Summer is the most straightforwardly pleasant of the year. It is the promise of early Spring beginning its fulfilment. The landscape still has its exhilarating freshness. Its variety of greens and profusion of growth have not yet settled into the rather stately affluent air of high Summer. Late Spring/early Summer is the time when Anglo-Saxon composure is most stirred by thoughts of Arcady, when we respond to the landscape in a pantheistic fashion, demonstrating for this short period an enthusiasm for life's physical beauty and a spontaneous joy at nature and in being a part of it.

But Summer as a whole is, popularly anyway, defined by joy—indeed how could it be otherwise given its physical attributes (in ideal manifestation of course). Brightness, growth, long days and so on offer almost limitless scope in the use of our leisure. Added to this is the fact that we all entertain Summer visions from childhood in which leisure was the main constituent, unconstrained by the rigors of the classroom, with a life of ease and adventure stretching before us, apparently to infinity, in weather always fair. . . . Indeed, the easing of constraints is what Summer allows us most, and the happiness we experience is due as much to this as to the actual conditions (although they are interdependent of course).

The knowledge that Summer will expire and pass into Autumn tends to concentrate the mind on its pleasures. People who leave the city—either for weekends or for their holidays, taking to the countryside or the coast—know they will have to return.

We cannot, in a gruesome Summer, behave with the alacrity we would in a splendid one. The association of Summer with holidays hardly needs mentioning but whatever holidays may constitute in the way of activities, they represent a relaxation of constraints— being excused readily, as it were, for a spell and allowed a freedom of movement which is inhibited at cooler times. I do not just mean the freedom to travel, although nowadays, paradoxically, that becomes increasingly more irksome; no, there are other freedoms Summer confers, perhaps more fundamental ones. For instance, we need to wear fewer and generally less formal clothes; our bodies work better for warmth and our minds tend to be more expansive and our eyes more acute. Also, the separation of indoors and out-of-doors is whittled away—our houses are no longer a protection from the elements but open to them; the garden functions as part of the house and vice versa and people spend as much time outside as they do inside.

However hard were the tasks that Summer brought in the past, the nature of life itself was made easier. Food was more plentiful, more varied; heating less urgent; roads passable and so on and the sun a more congenial companion than January rain. It is both sentimental and unrealistic to deplore the passing of what, to many people (usually of urban temperament) seem the good old days. What can, however, be counted as a legitimate source of sadness is that with their passing also passed much of the viability of rural life—a community with a logic to its existence, bound of necessity and with ties deeper than those of the cocktail party, the jumble sale and the resuscitation of rural crafts.

Finally, a confession, if one is needed. For, if the reader has got this far, he will have realized that my feelings as an artist toward Summer are not unequivocal. While I welcome its warmth and amplitude, I find it rather uninteresting to paint. Vivaldi's view of Summer as demonstrated in his set of violin concertos, *The Four Seasons*, leans toward the oppressive and is one I can easily share. But, unlike Vivaldi, and paying due respect to the gulf separating our respective talents, I seem unable or unconsciously unwilling to make songs about it. No, the other seasons would appear to entertain the muse on a more congenial if less comfortable stage.

78

Summer

Hannah, my younger daughter, bustling about the garden; she is determined, strong-willed and practical whereas Katie is introspective, not very practical, given to daydreams—all of which she displays with a robust sense of humor.

I had never drawn children before I came to parenthood at the age of 45. Two things occur to me, one, having them around makes them readily available as models, and two, your experience of them enables you to retrieve your own childhood to some extent.

The dictionary describes fête as "a festival, an entertainment on a large scale," and a fête champêtre as "an outdoor entertainment, a rural festival," so it is the latter that we would appear to hold. But, however it is defined, its origins presumably reach back to the unrecorded past. Probably it is those awesome mid-summer rites entered into by our distant ancestors to propitiate the sun in his season and which were taken over and transformed along more decorous lines by the Church. Indeed you could describe the atmosphere that fêtes give off as one of robust decorum.

As to the constituents of the average fête, these vary in direct proportion to the ambitions of the organizers. For example, in the year of the great drought, we had a Sea-Cadets' Marching Band—sweating band seemed nearer the mark if the pun can be forgiven. Some fêtes are opened by Members of Parliament, others by film stars or near celebrities from television, one was opened by the Duke of Norfolk. But whatever local variations there are, the essentials are the same. A mixture comprised of various amounts of duty, zeal, improvisation, contention, boredom and confusion.

Our fête is not, on the face of it, a "church fête," although the church is decorated with flowers most beautifully for the occasion, but it is organized on behalf of the village hall to provide funds for its maintenance. The hall itself is a prefabricated building, aesthetically negative or just worse, that was assembled eight years ago and serves the village in divers ways. My own part in these affairs has been small, usually limited to the production of notices reading "car park," "tombola," "pony rides," and so on—although, in the year of the drought and the Sea Scouts, I was deputized to watch the back entrance to stop those who had come across the fields from getting in without paying. Louise, on the other hand, is always nearer the center of things, organizing the children's pony rides.

The Village Fête

At every fête, no matter how elaborate or simple, certain incidents, I am sure, repeat themselves with little variation. For example, everything takes longer than has been anticipated; the parking of cars gets fouled up; key people, i.e., those who are to start a race, give out prizes, who have possession of a stop watch or are in receipt of small change, disappear when they are needed to render their services. The public address system either fails to issue a sound or whines like a tormented animal or, as was the case with us this year, works so well that the ear is battered until the mind becomes numbed with sound.

In among all this activity there are always lots of children, some of whom are silent, others noisy, or happy, or sad, distracted, excited, morose, and comatose—being pacified, reprimanded, cajoled, indulged, nursed, searched for and comforted. The general atmosphere is one of qualified good humor. If you look hard at a group of people at a fête—or anywhere else for that matter where the ostensible purpose is al fresco pleasure—you will find that few at any one moment actually appear to be enjoying themselves. On the other hand, for the day at least, a sort of tolerance reigns in everybody's breast, animosities are suspended, prejudices postponed until the fête is over and the money counted.

My eldest daughter, Katie, entered the fancy dress with her school friends, Ricky Bench and Keith Gent—they as a space man and Batman respectively, and she as a watersprite. For this impersonation, she wore a white dress scalloped round the skirt in spear-shaped fronds and girded with leaves and Christmas-tree tinsel. So dressed she won the second prize—the first going to a four-year-old butterfly. It was all too much for gentle Katie and she burst into deep sobs.

Our fête's attractions included children's fancy dress competitions, children's sports, pony rides, tombola, sales of work, stalls of local produce and the event that brought most visitors from outside the village—the tug-of-war competition.

A characteristic of fêtes is that they bring together all sorts of opposites—rich and poor, peer and commoner, young and old. I was struck by these two departures from the recreation ground—one a gentle progress toward the gate, the other a scramble over the Saxon rampart.

A view of the church looking towards the South-West.

Peter Bench, in serious vein. Peter bought the George & Dragon four years ago and runs it with his wife Jan, as a pub and restaurant—the halves divided by a curtain and a notice forbidding dogs and muddy boots.

Village Portraits

About the first thing you notice about George Gent is the blue of his eyes, made more intense by his high color—a deep brownish-red extending down his neck to where his shirt is buttoned—usually the third from the top. He is not tall and has a largish nose with a pronounced angle at the bridge, the record of a kick from a cow many years ago. His manner is watchful, at times verging on the suspicious, which will suddenly relax into mirth. On a few occasions when it was raining very hard, I have seen him with a mackintosh thrown over his shoulders. I've never seen him with an overcoat and only once with a tie on. He usually wears a cap, a sports jacket, grey trousers and, in the evening, plaid carpet slippers.

George has been in Burpham for twenty-eight years but only for the last four have he and his wife lived in the village itself. Before that he was the herdsman at Peppering High Barn, a post now occupied by his youngest son, Rodney. The High Barn is a bit out of the way, not isolated like Welsh hill farms for example, but then, isolation is relative and, for these parts, the High Barn is isolated. Indeed George's manner when he first moved down into the village itself was that of a man used to his own company. All his life he has worked with animals, first as a boy with teams of horses and later on a dairy farm in Wick near Littlehampton. Since that time until his retirement, cows, dogs and, to a lesser extent, horses, have been his life. But now his main activity is his garden. Apart from a part-time job tending the calves at Peppering Farm, he is very much what townspeople think of as a typical countryman—a bit taciturn, but friendly with a slightly mocking sense of humor. His life spans the revolution in farming from the days of horses to air-conditioned tractors and he himself seems to represent some of the virtues of the earlier way.

Until he retired two years ago, Jack Lloyd was the village's odd-job man as well as its beekeeper. He is a native of Wrexham in North Wales and came to Burpham during the war. Anybody who has trouble with almost anything from burst pipes to a cat on the roof rings Jack. He is a talkative man with strongly-affirmed opinions. He likes to "leaven" his work with intervals of conversation on any topic under the sun.

Jim Binfield comes from Hampshire, which is just detectable in his voice—probably the most stentorian in the village. It is difficult to imagine Jim whispering. For most of his twenty-eight years in Burpham, he worked at Peppering Farm as a shepherd (his old crooks are in the George & Dragon) but he retired from full-time farmwork four years ago. He is, I suppose, what tourists think of as a "real character"— come to think of it, he is what we think of as a "character" as well.

Although he is very much the village blacksmith, Stephen Jefford's work frequently takes him a fair distance away. He is shown here preparing to "cold-shoe" a horse.

Burpham's vicar, Canon Peter Schneider, is a friendly, talkative, approachable man, not at all narrow in his outlook. Czechoslovakia is not the first place you expect the vicar of a small Sussex parish to have been born—but that is, in fact, where he was born. He came to England as a boy just before the Second World War in which his parents perished. His schooling was finished here and, in 1949, he went to Fitzwilliam College, Cambridge, and was ordained in 1955—an event that was the culmination of an ambition first conceived at the age of eleven. In 1976 he came to Burpham after serving in various posts including a curacy in London, four years as Chaplain of Fitzwilliam College and, later, Canon at St. George's Cathedral in Jerusalem. The distance between Burpham and Jerusalem seems a negligible one to Canon Schneider. These are simply the two centers of his activity as a minister . . . the one, his parochial work, and the other his special interest in the relationship between the Christian and Jewish faiths—in this respect he is both secretary of the Consultants to the Archbishops of Canterbury and York on Interfaith Relations and a member of the board of international affairs of the British Council of Churches.

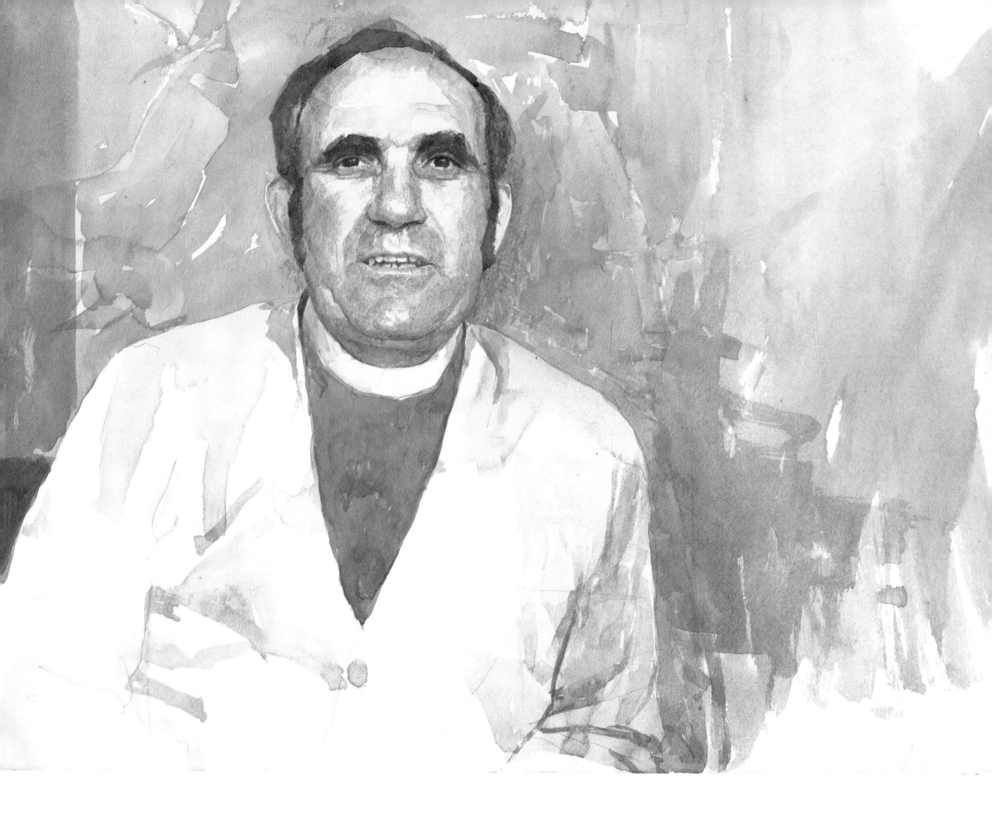

99

Summer Work

What, for the holidaymaker, is an idle hill, to the farmer is a field of barley. In fact Summer on the land is far from sleepy. It is the period of most intense activity. Haymaking and harvesting which, years ago, say up to the Second World War, occupied the labors of virtually the whole village—women and children as well as the men and both young and old—now fall to a handfull of skilled men operating expensive machinery. And, while the work is still intensive, still subject to the weather, and still fills the long daylight hours, it is impossible not to feel that something has been lost. The old gods of Summer do not preside easily over the combine harvester.

Tractor and combine in the barley field: the viewpoint is similar to the picture of rolling on page 59.

George driving the combine on Warre Field; the view is almost identical with the ploughing picture on page 57, and that water trough in the foreground is that on page 54.

George Field threading up the hay bales with twine.

The overseer! George with his arm in a sling—he was suffering from bursitis—looking at the bale escalator.

While George did the overseeing, Libby and daughter Sally got on with the strenuous task of loading bales of hay into the escalator leading to the hayloft.

Sally and Libby enjoying a well-earned rest.

Autumn

Autumn

If Spring is the season of energy and renewal, then Autumn could be called the season of replete tranquility. But, as I have said elsewhere in this book, whatever we believe, the essence of any season seems to be that it will always be something of an abstraction, or an ideal to which the caprices of reality hardly even conform. The opening lines of Keats' famous poem *To Autumn* represent just such an ideal:

> Season of mists and mellow fruitfulness
> Close bosom-friend of the maturing sun;

Calm, warm, abundant and glowingly colored—in a word, maturity. However, as in human life, the putative blessings of maturity can be illusory or, at best, deceptive, and Autumn, notwithstanding the attributes of its principal zodiacal sign, can dip depressingly low.

The most perfect Autumn imaginable is without peradventure the harbinger of Winter—its leaves may be red and gold, but they still fall by your window—their beauty intensified by their very mutability. Hence, I imagine, the two outstanding emotions that Autumn seems to induce in us—nostalgia and a kind of self-indulgent melancholy. Unlike Winter daydreams which tend to be anticipatory, Autumn reveries are retrospective, looking back to the Summer that has past.

I remember when, as a small boy (I was about eight I think), I stood in school assembly at the beginning of the Autumn term, profoundly miserable, mouthing the words of a lugubrious hymn while images of sand and shrimping nets occupied my mind almost obliterating the smell of linoleum, floor-polish and inkwells; such pleasures, I thought, are gone for good. That perhaps says more about my distaste for school than it does about anything to do with Autumn. But, since Summer is universally the time of warmth and relaxation, it is natural that it should be seen nostalgically from the viewpoint of its less frivolous, mature successor.

The painter John Everett Millais found his nostalgia triggered by leaves and bonfires to which he gave substance in his beautiful painting "Autumn Leaves." This depicts four soulful, well-bred little girls making, almost ceremoniously, a pile of leaves against a landscape of a waxing afternoon. Some years before he painted this, however, he is alleged to have expressed himself on the subject to his Pre-Raphaelite colleague Holman Hunt. "Is there," he asked, "any sensation more delicious than that awakened by the odor of burning leaves? To me nothing brings back sweeter memories of the days that are gone; it is the incense offered by departing summer to the sky and it brings on a happy conviction that time puts a peaceful seal on all that is gone." On the same theme, such glowing, not to say childish optimism is not shared by Thomas Hardy in his poem *Autumn in King's Hintock Park*—nor would one expect it. An old woman whose

115

task it is to rake the fallen leaves speculates on the indifference of nature to our feelings. The final resigned stanza runs:

> Yet, Dear, though one may sigh,
>   Raking up leaves,
> New leaves will dance on high—
>   Earth never grieves!
> Will not, when missed am I
>   Raking up leaves.

Leaves again figure in the less fettered, more overtly passionate mood of Shelley's verse:

> O wild west wind, thou breath of Autumn's being,
> Thou, from whose unseen presence the leaves dead
> Are driven, like ghosts from an enchanter fleeing.

> Yellow, and black, and pale and hectic red . . .

The poem goes on to describe the leaves lying "cold and low/each like a corpse within its grave," a long way from Millais' "delicious," "sweeter memories." It would be tempting to confess that it was feelings such as Shelley describes that led me to paint the two pictures of our churchyard in Autumn, but I am afraid it was not so—certainly not consciously anyway. Yet when I was working on them in the studio, a connection between the fallen leaves, destined to become earth, and the lichen and headstones marking remains that have long since been so transformed, stuck in my mind. But I cannot say in what way the look of the pictures might materially have been affected.

Whether you regard autumn leaves as tokens of an idyllic past or of maturity, or of death and decay, they are the inescapable symbols of the season and their spectacular color is its most characteristic aspect. For me the first signs of gold and russet in the trees are, whatever their portent, a refreshing and stimulating sight—a marvelous restorative after the flaccid green of late Summer.

Burpham Church

The church was, traditionally, the pivot of the village—not just the building itself but the institution; the place where all classes and all trades came together in the equality of worship. Through the rites of baptism, marriage and burial, it saw the lives of the inhabitants in and out, and in the person of the vicar the village possessed an influence which balanced secular authority. Today the role of the church is less comprehensive and more, if you like, professional, in that the rites alone of the church's functions are in demand—it is the only place to be baptized, the soundest place to be married and the wisest place to be buried. Consequently it is not the unifying factor it once was but it is probably true to say that the country church is still closer to the lives of the people than is the church of an urban or suburban parish. Perhaps in the country the essential patterns of existence are more easily apprehended than in the town—the movement of the seasons is more directly observable and the presence of animals is a good introduction to and a constant reminder of the nature of mortality.

Of course, people go to church for all sorts of reasons, some of them having little to do with religious belief in the fundamental sense. The church is a symbol of the relatively unchanging in a changing world and its liturgy is often seen more as a connection with secure, remembered past than the straightforward expression of faith. Even without heaven, the purely human values the church represents seem to be having a lean time of it in the world as it is today constituted. My own position, which I feel bound to declare at this point, is that of a sympathetic non-believer which means in practice that I, like a lot of people who do not attend services, cannot accept what is fundamental—I love churches for themselves, as buildings, as repositories of local history, as accessible links with the past and as places dedicated to something other than material progress.

The vicar, like his church, plays a diminished role in today's society. Instead of being, with the squire, one of the key figures in village life, there is a tendency to regard him as just another professional who, at certain times, performs professional tasks for people who otherwise seek nothing of him. In this sense he is less isolated, less a separate figure than his predecessors were and his cloth is less awesome although it still carries authority. Notice, for example, how the demeanor of people in a pub changes when a clergyman enters—even that of the most vociferous materialist.

A view from the garden of Splash Farm.

The River Arun at the bottom of Warre Field.

The river flowing below the railway bridge near
Peppering Farm.

The Dryer Lane
Winter Barley coming through

Machinery at Peppering Farm which I feel is very much a part of the landscape and as familiar and somehow ageless as the hills, trees, and meadows.

The side of the Dryer barn with part of Perry Hill, one of the two corrugated asbestos additions to the original barn, and the very new grain-drying siloes. There is a popular view that anything to do with the 20th century is an intrusion into the landscape. Such a view seems to be quite false.

The Dryer Barn on a frosty morning. This is my
favorite complex of farm buildings in the area and
has served me with material for more paintings than
anything else. The buildings increase in modernity
from left to right—the original barn on the left is
dated 1838, whereas the chateau-like grain silo is
only a few years old.

Back view of the main barn at Burpham High Barn
(or the Dryer Barn). I was attracted by the constant
adaptation to new conditions, such as the juxtaposition
of the dryer exhausts set into the flintwork.

The old dairy at Peppering High Barn where the milk churns, in the days when such things were used, were put out for collection. The building has been renovated since this drawing was made.

A view from Peppering High Barn
looking towards Arundel Castle
and the sea beyond.

South, from the recreation field

Jackson's Barn - late Autumn.

Right →
One of the cottages
at Peppering High Barn
looking towards Perry Hill

Little Down

This view of my house from the paddock, with the western end of Perry Hill in the background, is the one I see during the time every morning of the year when I feed, water and muck out our two ponies. This transition time equates, I suppose, with the period office workers spend traveling to work.

The separation of work and home is very necessary when you work at home. It is very hard simply to push your coffee cup aside and reach for the brushes. The face that my break involves tending to the animals is doubly rewarding—in itself and because contact with animals is a reassuring one, providing an immediate sense of reality (always a valuable quality to any artist forced by the nature of his work to spend long periods of time alone). On top of that, there is the lack of choice. Having to go out in any weather forces you to make the best of it and very often that is much better than you could ever imagine. I'm sure it is this, as much as anything in my nature, that enables me to enjoy "bad" weather and to paint "bad weather" paintings.

The house itself was once a potting-shed and, some time later, an apple store. I tell myself you can still smell the apples. Originally, with the cottage next door, it was part of the outbuildings of the then vicarage (now the Burpham Country Hotel situated to the left out of the picture). The upper floor was added in the 1930's, in a very functional ad hoc manner with eccentric fenestration, by its owner and an odd-job man.

I like the appearance of roofs, particularly from higher ground when their color and texture "reads" more clearly than when seen against the brightness of the sky. This was the primary reason for painting the picture. There are two reasons for painting anything; one, because of what it looks like, and the other because of what it is. Most pictures are the outcome of some combination of the two. You can, for example, be so involved with the appearance of a thing—its shape, color, texture—that the significance of its identity is of little account. But equally, you can start at the opposite extreme and work, as it were, toward the middle—if you are lucky—for that is the area in which most good paintings occur.

With this picture, it was the roof against the hillside and the pattern of the trees against the virtually windowless wall that made me begin. But the fact that it was *my* house, and not just any house, turned it in method closer to that of a portrait. I'm very fond of that frieze of sumac trees on the edge of the paddock, despite being told that they are alien—Chinese trees somebody said. According to my encyclopedia, they are North American—*Rhus typhina*. The point is that while I would never have planted them myself (ash or beech would have filled that choice), having inherited them, so to speak, I can like them very much. In the same way I can like the name of the house too—Little Down—with the knowledge that it is not one I would have chosen (I prefer numbers) and, since the hotel is called The Old Down and my neighbors' cottage, once the stables, Down Cottage, the name of Little Down for our old potting-shed has a kind of logic.

137

The End of the Year

The trouble with seeing the world through the seasons is that they are so variable. We anticipate them in their most typical manifestations, summer-hot, autumn-gold and so on, but so often the actual experience is a long way from the model. Yet whichever way a particular season chooses to present itself to us, and however the details of our lives are affected by this sunny day or that misty one, there seems to be a consistent response to Autumn which is simply part review and part anticipation: a backward, nostalgic gaze at the past Summer and an apprehensive glance at the coming Winter. This forward and backward character which acts on our emotions is also rooted in our physical needs, for what goes on in our heads goes on as well in the ground, literally, in the clearing, and tidying, and securing in preparation for Winter.

These physical effects of Autumn, it is almost unnecessary to remark, are virtually unnoticed in the city, apart perhaps from the smoke of burning leaves in the suburbs—although I have to say that I do remember from my years in London some dazzling displays of autumnal colour in Hyde Park, Kensington Gardens and the other oases of green with which London is so liberally provided. What I mean is that while, in a city, our senses may be touched, the details of our clothes affected and our habits modified by season and weather, the actual course of our lives remains the same. The year unfolds, bringing inconvenience or pleasure, sunshine or artificial light but the city and its momentum persist and our reasons for being in it remain the same.

In the country things are rather different, or perhaps I should say things used to be different and are now only different in certain respects. However, the legacy of any earlier essential difference still colours many aspects of life in the country—it is, I suppose, a manner of perceiving nature and of reacting to its changes rather than any physical demands made. But those physical demands, though less elemental than, say, Thomas Hardy's natives labouring in the driving rain, are real enough even with today's highly organised and industrialised farming. Farm work in Autumn still conveys, to me at least, the character of urgent preparation for Winter, particularly the sight and sound of tractors rumbling all day over the wide chalk fields as they first plough, then drill the winter barley which will lie in the ground through the long cold months.

The changing seasons, of course, bring changes to the social life of the village, as, indeed, they do in town. It is simply that in a small village the changes are more noticeable, just as the weather itself is more noticeable because you can see more of it.

Storm-clouds rolling from horizon to horizon affect the mind more profoundly than when glimpsed in a rectangular patch above the city street, although the consequences of their issue are far more irksome if you are walking down Oxford Street than if you are on the Downs.

Oddly enough, one of the surest signs that Autumn is beginning to slip slowly into Winter is social rather than natural, and that is the diminishing number of visitors, tourists, walkers and the like about the village and the Downs, especially about the pub. Throughout the summer months visitors can be seen with the Ploughman's Lunches and pints of beer sitting at the outside tables or else picnicking on the rectangular ground in the shelter of the Saxon rampart. In the evenings too, people drive up from the coast for drinks or a meal, filling the bar with strange, often red, faces, and casual clothes. Like the swallows they are part of Summer and as reliably they depart; the date varies of course, depending on the weather, but when the last has left you know that Winter is not that far away.

Our village street is never what you could call populous, but in Summer the hikers, and the parties of school children, and the tourists on their way to the pub's restaurant, give the appearance of leisure and of fête-like pleasures. Of course, during the winter months people still come up on fine days to look at the landscape, or for a drink in a comfortable country pub, and occasionally the dedicated walker in anorak and boots is to be seen on the Downs. So the restaurant is still patronized (fortunately, for it helps keep the pub in business) but the frivolity and expansiveness associated with summer holidays is missing.

Visitors, tourists, whatever you call them, are regarded rather ambivalently by some of us—not exactly unwelcome, not exactly welcome either. I personally like to see them. I go to other places where I am a tourist and if you live in a place that is regarded as beautiful you simply have to share it. And tourists do have the positive effect that their interest tends to renew our own awareness of and response to the landscape we live with year round.

Their going, like the falling of the leaves, the final cricket match of the season, smoke rising from chimneys at first light, horses starting their winter coats—all are signs of the beginning of the end of the year when the mood not only of the village but of the surroundings as well becomes introspective as it were, and the sense of loneliness, never very far away in the country, becomes intensified in the empty landscape that waits, as we do, for another Winter.

Roger Coleman went to Leicester College of Art in 1947 with no clear idea what aspect of art he wanted to study, knowing only that drawing had been his best subject in school.

His first predeliction as an art student was for sculpture and for the first two years it seemed that this is what he would pursue. However, some combination of circumstances, the details of which he has forgotten, decided him to specialize in painting. His tastes at the time revolved round English romantic landscape-based artists such as Sutherland, Paul Hardy, Keith Vaughan and John Piper. At the same time he began what was to become a lifetime's preoccupation with the representation of the human face. Indeed most of his spare time away from the life and compulsory classes at the college was spent in persuading friends and relations and friends' relatives to sit long hours while he examined and painted their faces. One such picture, of a friend's brother, won him a national competition designed to encourage the creative revival of portrait painting. By this time he had gained entrance to the Royal College of Art for a further three years post-graduate study and it seemed to him then, and to his colleagues and teachers as well, that he would concentrate on portrait painting.

But all plans, particularly those assumed without much practical investigation, have a habit of being scuttled by experience. Before anything further could be pursued there was National Service to be undergone, consequently the next two years were spent in the Royal Artillery on the borders of Wales waiting for the days to pass while anticipating life in London and the Royal College of Art.

The long awaited time arrived—and passed. At the end of three years' painting at the Royal College of Art Coleman was both less sure of his ability and certainly less sure of the direction he ought to take than he had been while anticipating those years from an army camp in Shropshire. But a direction was provided by his being given a year's stint as full-time editor of the college's journal *Ark*. At this time the art world was at the beginnings of an enormous change largely under the impact of the 'new American painting' which was being shown in London for the first time. Sides were taken, and tempers were heated in discussions about the work of painters such as Jackson Pollock, Willem de Kooning, Mark Rothko and so on. The centre of much of the support for the new painting was the Institute of Contemporary Arts, the exhibitions committee of which Coleman was invited to join.

After his year as an editor, during which he had done little or no painting, Coleman was offered an editorial job on the magazine *Design*, the journal of *The Design Centre* in London, an offer he accepted because, as he said to a friend at the time, he could not think of a reason for saying no, and anyway he was not actually painting with feverish enthusiasm. So the following five years were spent on writing, criticism, lecturing and arranging exhibitions. One of the areas of study at the ICA at this time was that of the popular arts, as they were rather solemnly called then—today it would be called Media Studies or something more modest. What it meant in practice was that such popular visual and sound manifestations as TV, advertising, science-fiction art, pop music and jazz were analyzed and discussed with the kind of intensity and seriousness that had hitherto been reserved for say Rembrandt's treatment of the Old Testament or the use of ornament in Neo-Classic architecture. It is not perhaps surprising in the light of this, that when Coleman began to want to draw again it was towards the mass-media that he was attracted rather than the ambience of the art gallery. And as a result of such chance arrangements of events that can never be planned for, he eventually found himself as a full-time illustrator, painting paperback covers, magazine illustrations, industrial reportage, sports pictures, especially of football, and so on.

Through the 1960's he lived in London and worked from a studio in premises shared with several colleagues in Soho. In 1970 he met Louise, his wife, who was then the flat-mate of a girl who worked for his agent. After they married they lived in London until moving to Burpham in 1972.